BANKRUPTCY

D. M. Macarthur, *LL.B.*

LAW TEXTS FOR STUDENTS—V

THE ACCOUNTANTS' PUBLISHING CO. LTD. *for*

The Institute of Chartered Accountants of Scotland

27 QUEEN STREET, EDINBURGH EH2 1LA

First printed November 1970

LAW TEXTS FOR STUDENTS

Other titles in this series:—

I **The Law of Contract**
R. A. Bennett, Q.C., M.A., LL.B.

II **Sale of Goods, Trade Descriptions & Hire Purchase**
J. Casey, M.A., LL.B., F.I.ARB.
J. B. Stewart, M.A., LL.B.

III **Negotiable Instruments**
Professor J. Bennett Miller, T.D., M.A., LL.B.

IV **Arbitration**
Professor J. Bennett Miller, T.D., M.A., LL.B.

Forthcoming:—

VI **Succession, Trusts & Judicial Factors**
I. B. Rodger, LL.B.

VII **Agency, Insurance & Cautionary Obligations**
J. L. M. Mitchell, M.A., LL.B.

VIII **Partnership**
I. M. S. Robertson, B.L., N.P.

SBN 85099 010 6

Contents

INTRODUCTION

The modern Scots law of bankruptcy is codified in the Bankruptcy (Scotland) Act 1913 and, unless otherwise specified, references are to this Act.

The main principle underlying the law of bankruptcy is that when a man becomes insolvent he shall be required to hand over his whole estate to his creditors for distribution among them in accordance with their rights and claims, and thereafter be discharged of all claims which existed when he became insolvent.

In the early history of Scots law a debtor could only obtain his discharge by actual payment or by the favour of his creditors. Imprisonment for debt was competent, and the debtor could only secure his release or prevent his imprisonment by the process of *cessio bonorum*, *i.e.* by the giving up of his whole estate to his creditors. This, however, did not bind creditors who were not cited in the process, and the debtor did not obtain discharge from any debts which were not satisfied in full.

Sequestration was first introduced by the Bankrupts Act 1772, which was confined to debtors who were alive and engaged in trade but was subsequently extended to include all debtors living and the estates of deceased debtors. The Bankruptcy (Scotland) Act 1913 abolished *cessio bonorum*.

One result of the harshness of the early law towards debtors was that it encouraged fraud. A debtor might attempt to rid himself of his remaining assets by giving them gratuitously or in trust to relatives, or by conveying them as preferences to favoured creditors, and the Bankruptcy Act 1621 (cap. 18) was introduced to check these abuses. The Bankruptcy Act 1696 (cap. 5) laid down conditions to determine a state of public or notour bankruptcy, and declared that all deeds for the payment or further security of prior creditors granted within 60 days of such notour bankruptcy, or at any time subsequent thereto, should be deemed to be fraudulent and of no effect. These two Acts remain of great practical importance.

The Act of 1913 makes no limit to those persons who may be made notour bankrupt, and accordingly every person who is liable for debt may be rendered notour bankrupt.

A—INSOLVENCY

Throughout this text the terms " insolvency " and " notour bankruptcy " will be used frequently, but it must be appreciated that they do not admit of precise legal definition.

Insolvency is the more extensive term and may be used to describe either simple insolvency or public insolvency, *i.e.* " notour bankruptcy ", as it is styled. Simple insolvency merely indicates the condition of a person who is unable to pay his debts. Notour bankruptcy is a condition or status fixed by statute which implies public notice of insolvency and must be constituted in the prescribed manner. Bankruptcy is commonly used as a generic term and may mean any of three things:—

(1) simple insolvency;

(2) notour bankruptcy; or

(3) bankruptcy in the sense that the insolvent has handed over his estate to a trustee for the benefit of the general body of creditors.

Insolvency may be shown to exist in a *practical* or an *absolute* sense. Practical insolvency means that a debtor does not have the assets to meet his debts as and when they become due, even although he might be able to do so, given time. This is insolvency in the ordinary language of commerce. It may be indicated by failure to meet a bill or pay a liquid debt, by the granting of a mandate for sequestration or by the calling of a meeting of creditors. Section 62 (3), Sale of Goods Act 1893 provides that " a person is deemed to be insolvent within the meaning of this Act who has either ceased to pay his debts in the ordinary course of business, or cannot pay his debts as they become due, whether he has committed an act of bankruptcy or not, and whether he has become a notour bankrupt or not ".

Absolute insolvency means that on a given date a debtor's assets are exceeded by the amount of his liabilities. This is a significant situation in that from the time he becomes aware of the fact the debtor must act as a trustee for his creditors. He may continue his trade or profession, but everything must be done in the ordinary course of business. The debtor may continue to enter contracts, borrow money or grant securities with a view to effecting a recovery in his fortunes.[1]

Insolvency may alter the rights and obligations of parties in contracts such as those of sale, partnership or lease. It would for instance entitle a creditor who was due to deliver goods under a contract to exercise retention against the debtor.

[1] *Ehrenbacher & Co.* v. *Kennedy* (1874) 1 R. 1131.

B—NOTOUR BANKRUPTCY

Insolvency is a question of fact, not a legal condition. The debtor's own knowledge imposes certain duties on him, but only when his inability to meet his obligations becomes public does it affect bankruptcy procedure and at this stage the debtor is said to be notour bankrupt.

Notour bankruptcy is a state created by statute, and the conditions required for its constitution are laid down by section 5 of the 1913 Act. These are:—

(1) *Sequestration*, or the issuing of an adjudication of bankruptcy or any comparable order in England or Ireland: sequestration may be at the instance of the creditors or of the debtor himself, although in the latter case creditors' consent will be necessary; or

(2) *Insolvency*, concurrent with—

(*a*) a duly executed charge for payment, and the expiry of the days of charge;

(*b*) the lapse of the time which must pass before poinding or imprisonment, where a charge is not necessary;

(*c*) poinding of the debtor's moveables for non-payment of rates and taxes;

(*d*) decree of adjudication of any part of the debtor's heritable estate for payment or in security; or

(*e*) a sale of any of the debtor's effects under a sequestration for rent.

For the purposes of section 5, insolvency is practical insolvency, *i.e.* a present inability to meet debts when due.[2] Under section 6, relating to firms, the notour bankruptcy of a firm (called in the Act a " company ") may be constituted in any of the foregoing ways or by any of the partners being rendered notour bankrupt for a debt owed by the firm. Companies registered under the Companies Acts cannot be sequestrated but would be subject to liquidation proceedings.

The Duration of Notour Bankruptcy (section 7)

Notour bankruptcy is constituted when the above mentioned requisites occur, and when constituted it will continue, in the case of a

[2] *Scottish Milk Marketing Board* v. *Wood* 1936 S.C. 604.

sequestration, until the debtor obtains his discharge and in other cases until insolvency ceases. Notour bankruptcy may be constituted a second time while a previous period of notour bankruptcy is unexpired or after the expiry thereof and any second or subsequent constitution is available for purposes of equalisation of diligence or application for sequestration.

The Effects of Notour Bankruptcy

(1) *Equalisation of arrestments and poindings* (*section 10*)

It was not until the Bankrupts Act 1772 that the acquisition of preferences by creditors was checked by a provision that arrestments or poindings executed within 30 days of sequestration should be void. The relevant provisions are now contained in section 10 of the 1913 Act. All arrestments and poindings used within the 60 days prior to the constitution of notour bankruptcy or within four months thereafter shall rank *pari passu* or equally as if they had all been used at the same date. If such an arrestment is made on the dependence of an action it must, to be allowed to rank, be followed up without undue delay. If a creditor then judicially produces in a process relative to such an arrestment on the dependence either liquid grounds of debt or a decree for payment, then he is entitled to rank as if he had executed an ordinary arrestment or poinding. If one creditor recovers payment, then, subject to the deduction of his expenses, he must share the proceeds with all creditors whose diligences are equalised. Any arrestments used after the expiry of the four months subsequent to bankruptcy will not compete with those used during or prior to the periods mentioned, but may rank on any reversion of the funds attached. If sequestration is awarded, the trustee ranks equally with creditors who had executed arrestments or poindings within 60 days (sections 103 and 104). If sequestration does not occur within four months of the constitution of notour bankruptcy the user of diligence within the terms of section 10 will give a good title in a question with the trustee.

(2) *The availability of sequestration proceedings* (*section 11*)

This is the second important consequence of notour bankruptcy. Sequestration may be awarded in the case of living debtors subject to the jurisdiction of the Supreme Courts of Scotland as follows:—

(*a*) on the debtor's own petition, with the concurrence of a creditor or creditors duly qualified; and

(*b*) on the petition of a creditor or creditors duly qualified, provided the debtor be notour bankrupt and, within a year before the date of the presentation of the petition, have resided or had a dwelling-house or a place of business in Scotland. Section 13 provides that such petitions, presented without the concurrence of the debtor, shall be competent only if brought within four months of the constitution of notour bankruptcy. In the case of a deceased debtor no sequestration shall be awarded within six months of the date of death, unless there was notour bankruptcy at that date or the debtor's successor has renounced the succession.

Gratuitous Alienations

In considering absolute insolvency (see page 2) it was observed that the insolvent was not prevented from carrying on his trade or business. Generally, however, any transaction not within the ordinary course of business may be challenged either as a gratuitous alienation or as a fraudulent preference. It has been recognised as a general principle of Scots law that, if while he is insolvent a debtor prejudices his creditors by a voluntary alienation of his property, then his conduct will be considered to be fraud. From the moment of insolvency a debtor is bound to act as a mere trustee, or rather as the *negotiorum gestor*, of his creditors, who have from that time an exclusive interest in his funds. The debtor may continue to trade with a view to making a gain for his creditors and himself, but as his funds are no longer his own he is not entitled to set apart anything for himself or to give assets away capriciously.[3] In the case of an insolvent debtor, to render a transfer liable to challenge creditors will require only to satisfy themselves of the existence of insolvency, and that no valuable consideration was received by the debtor. Any form of transfer, whether by direct conveyance, indirect operation, written deed or simple delivery, may be challenged. So, where an insolvent gave his sister £500, and this was placed on deposit receipt, an action against the sister for reduction of the deposit receipt was held to be competent.[4] A challenge will cover the alienation of any kind of right which could otherwise be made available for the benefit of creditors, *e.g.* policies of insurance effected by a debtor on his life, or the assignation of a lease, or an interest in a trust estate. The essential basis of any challenge is the fraud of the debtor, *i.e.* his breach of the implied trust for his creditors. Fraud in its broadest sense (implying a contrivance or scheme between the debtor and a third party) does not require to be present: during

[3] BELL: *Comm. II*, 170.
[4] *Dobie* v. *Mitchell* (1854) 17 D. 97.

insolvency a gratuitous alienation is presumed to be fraudulent and proof of intention is not necessary. Further, knowledge by the grantee of the grantor's insolvency is not material. The motives of either party to the transfer are not significant in setting up a challenge as valid.

The conditions justifying the challenge at common law of the transfer of the property of an insolvent may be summarised thus:—

(1) the alienation must be voluntary and gratuitous: it is not so if consideration is received or if it is made to implement a prior obligation;

(2) the debtor must have been absolutely insolvent at the time of the alienation and of the challenge: the challenger must offer proof that the debtor's liabilities were, on a fair estimate, in excess of his assets; and

(3) the alienation must have prejudiced the challenger. It is sufficient for this purpose that the challenger show that the effect of the transfer has been to put property otherwise available for division beyond the reach of the creditors. Any onerous creditor may make the challenge whether his debt was incurred before or after the date of the alienation.

There are four main effects of a successful challenge:—

(1) the alienation is reduced only so far as the challenging creditor is prejudiced, and other creditors whose claims are prior to the date of the alienation can use diligence on the property released;

(2) preferences over the particular property by diligence before sequestration are not affected;

(3) a third party who has acquired the property for a fair value and in good faith from the debtor's grantee is not affected; and

(4) if the trustee in the debtor's sequestration is the successful challenger, the alienation is wholly reduced and the estate vested in him accordingly increased.

It may often be difficult to prove that an alienation by an insolvent debtor was in fact gratuitous or that the debtor was actually insolvent, and therefore challenges are generally made not on the basis of the common law but in reliance on the provisions of the Bankruptcy Act 1621 (cap. 18). This Act provides that all alienations made by a debtor " to any conjunct and confident person without true just and necessary causes, and without a just price really payed, the same being done after the contracting of lawful debts from true creditors " shall be null when challenged by the creditors injured. The main purpose of the Act was to prevent fraud, and two valuable presumptions have been established by judicial interpretation of it:

(1) that the alienation was made without onerous consideration; and

(2) that the debtor's insolvency existed at the time of making the alienation.

" Conjunct " persons are those who have a near relationship to the insolvent by blood or affinity. " Confident " persons are those who stand in a position of trust to the insolvent, such as masters, servants, partners in business or professional advisers. If the grantor claims he is solvent *at the date of the challenge*, the challenging creditor will require to prove insolvency; if the creditor does so, insolvency *at the date of alienation* is presumed.

According to the Act the challenge may come " from any true creditor ", and this is generally taken to mean a creditor whose ground of debt is prior to the alienation. Posterior creditors may otherwise have the benefit of the Act.[5]

It is a good answer to a challenge that the alienation was granted for some true, just and necessary cause.

As under the common law, if a single creditor has made a successful challenge, the deed is cut down to the extent that it is prejudicial to that creditor. Where the challenge is by the trustee in bankruptcy the benefit is made available to all creditors, and third parties acquiring for value and in good faith are protected again as under the common law.

Fraudulent Preferences

Voluntary preferences granted by insolvent debtors to creditors are also open to challenge. Unlike the gratuitous donee, a creditor has a legal claim on his debtor, and in obtaining settlement or some form of security the creditor is in a sense only getting his due. The reason for challenging the voluntary preference is that it is an interference with the rights of the creditors among themselves once the debtor is insolvent.

The Bankruptcy Act 1696 (cap. 5) provides " All and whatsoever voluntar dispositions assignations or other deeds which shall be

[5] Sections 8 and 9, Bankruptcy (Scotland) Act 1913.

found to be made and granted directly or indirectly, by the foresaid dyvor [debtor] or bankrupt either at or after his becoming bankrupt or in the space of 60 days and before in favour of his creditors, either for their satisfaction or in further security, in preference to other creditors to be void and null ". The period of 60 days is now extended to six months by section 115 (3), Companies Act 1947.

As the insolvent retains power to continue his business in the ordinary course *and for full value*, insolvency does not debar him from granting security for advances to be made to him, or from making payment to a creditor in cash, provided the payment is due and not fraudulent.

A direct preference may be given by disposition, assignation, endorsation of a bill of exchange or simply by delivery of moveable property in extinction of or as security for a debt. An indirect preference may be given by abandoning a defence to an action or by the granting of a document of title for a hitherto unconstituted debt. The document must create a preference, and a mere acknowledgment of an existing debt will not be struck at. Although the basis of the statute is fraud, the challenger need not prove the debtor's intention to defraud his creditors.

Transactions Voluntary and in Satisfaction or Security of Prior Debt

The transaction must in all cases have been in favour of a *creditor* of the insolvent, and gratuitous transfers do not come within the scope of the 1696 Act. The legislature did not intend to prevent insolvents from implementing their obligations as these became due, but from favouring individual creditors to the prejudice of the general body of creditors by anticipating due payment or by the transference of assets in security of the prior debt.[6] Specific implement of an obligation *ad factum praestandum* is not viewed as a voluntary deed.

There are three classes of transactions acknowledged to be outside the scope of the Act:—

(1) *Cash payments*

Cash payments of debts currently due are regarded simply as the satisfaction of an existing obligation. Cash payments will include payment in bank notes, or by cheques drawn by the debtor, bankers' drafts or any mercantile documents which can be immediately exchanged for cash. Payment by a bill of exchange or by endorsed cheque will be struck at unless proved to be in the ordinary course

[6] *Taylor* v. *Farrie* (1855) 17 D. 639.

of business. Payments must be *bona fide*, and transfers of cash before payment is due will be regarded as payments in security.

(2) *Transactions in the ordinary course of trade*

Transactions between a debtor and his creditor in the ordinary course of trade are treated as an exception to the Act in the same way as cash payments. Otherwise commercial practice would be completely disrupted. Whether a transaction falls within this category will depend on the circumstances of each particular case. Delivery of goods in implement of a contract will fall within this exception. Payments by endorsation of bills are *prima facie* struck at.

(3) *Nova debita*

A *novum debitum* is an obligation undertaken by the bankrupt in respect of some present consideration received, *e.g.* delivery of goods for a price paid, or a loan of money on a specific security given by the bankrupt. The implement of such obligations does not create a preference or grant further security, since for what is given a corresponding benefit accrues to the insolvent's estate. Moreover, there has been no prior relationship of debtor and creditor to bring the transaction within the scope of the statute. *Nova debita* are not necessarily obligations undertaken within the days of bankruptcy. The performance of the obligation need not be simultaneous with its formation.

C—SEQUESTRATION

Sequestration involves an application to the court for authority to take the debtor's assets out of his hands and transfer them to a trustee for ultimate division among the creditors.

In the case of *living* debtors the debtor himself must be subject to the jurisdiction of the Supreme Courts of Scotland (section 11, Bankruptcy Act 1913), and the application must be at the instance of the debtor with the concurrence of a duly qualified creditor or creditors or at the instance of such creditors alone. The " qualification " is a debt or debts amounting to not less than £50, either liquid or illiquid, but not contingent (*i.e.* conditional on the occurrence of some future event) (section 12). The petition may be presented to the Court of Session, or to the Sheriff Court within whose jurisdiction the debtor either resided or carried on business within one year of the presentation of the petition. If the award is made in the Court of Session the case is remitted to the appropriate Sheriff Court for further procedure. Where the debtor presents the petition the only requisites are jurisdiction and the necessary consents. Where the petition is at the instance of creditors they must establish that the debtor was notour bankrupt within four months of the presentation and that within one year the debtor has resided or has had a place of business within the jurisdiction of the Court (section 13).

In the case of *deceased* debtors the sequestration is simply a process of distribution and does not imply that the deceased was bankrupt or even insolvent. It enables creditors who have been unable to obtain payment to take the management of the estate into their own hands by judicial authority. The debtor must have been subject to the jurisdiction of the Supreme Courts of Scotland at his death and the petition must be at the instance of either a duly qualified creditor or of a mandatory of the debtor (section 11 (2)). Although the petition may be presented at any time, no award will be made until six months have expired from the date of death, unless the debtor was notour bankrupt on his death or his successors concur in the petition and renounce the succession (section 13). Similar provisions relate to companies other than registered companies.

The Petitioning Creditor

The rules which determine the competency of a person to sue in an ordinary action determine the competency of a petition for sequestration. Joint creditors must petition jointly. In the case of corporations the " responsible officer " appointed to represent the company must petition in his own name.

The petitioning creditor's debt

The debt or debts must total £50, and interest accrued, if allowed by law or under contract, may be included to the date of the petition. Claims for damages are really contingent on the establishment of liability and will not support a petition. Any debt which has been affected by the expiry of any of the prescriptive periods applicable to it may not be used.

The Petition

Section 16 provides which are the competent courts to award sequestration, as noticed in connection with the provisions of section 11. If the requirements of residence or of carrying on of business cannot be satisfied in one sheriffdom, the application must be made in the Court of Session. No court will award sequestration if it is proved that another court has made an award which has not been discharged. If a petition is in course of consideration by one court, a petition in a second court will probably be remitted to the first court. Usually the second petition will be sisted until a decision is reached on the first. If the petition is not signed by the petitioner but by his counsel or agent, a mandate authorising the application must be produced (section 20). It need not be in any special form but must be unambiguous in its terms. Where the debtor grants a mandate and dies before the petition has been presented, the mandatory may proceed. If the debtor dies after the presentation of the petition, the instance falls.

Style of petition

There is no special style of petition, and the form has been regulated by practice. If the petition is brought by the debtor it should narrate that he is subject to the jurisdiction of the appropriate court and that the concurring creditor or creditors are duly qualified, and it should crave the grant of sequestration. If the petition is brought by a creditor without the concurrence of the debtor it must narrate the creditor's qualification, that the debtor has been made notour bankrupt within *four* months and continues in that state, and that he is subject to the jurisdiction. Presentation of, or concurrence in, a petition for sequestration, or lodging a claim, interrupts the running of prescription on the creditor's debt.

The Oath or Affidavit

The petitioning or concurring creditor must produce along with the petition an oath or affidavit as to the verity of the debt, with the vouchers necessary to prove it (section 20). Section 21 specifies the nature and contents of the oath, which must—

(1) state the persons, if any, other than the bankrupt, liable for the debt or any part thereof;

(2) state the nature and extent of any security held, or any co-obligants;

(3) state that there are no obligants or securities other than those specified;

(4) state, if such is the case, that no person other than the bankrupt is bound and no security is held; and

(5) specify, in the case of a deceased debtor, his last residence or place of business (section 23).

The creditor is not required to value the securities, and the vouchers need only adduce *prima facie* evidence of the debt. Where the petition is at the instance of creditors, evidence of notour bankruptcy, generally an expired charge, must be produced.

The Award of Sequestration

Where the court is satisfied that the foregoing procedural requirements have been satisfied, it will issue a deliverance awarding sequestration of the debtor's estate, and any estate which he may acquire before discharge, and declaring that the estate will belong to the creditors for the purpose of the Act (section 28). If the petition is presented without the concurrence of the debtor, or he is deceased, the court will grant warrant to cite the debtor or his successor to appear and show why sequestration should not be granted (section 25). The *induciae* of citation (the period between the date of the warrant of citation and the date of appearance) will be not less than six and not more than fourteen days (section 27). The court will also order intimation of the warrant and diet of appearance in the EDINBURGH GAZETTE. When the advertisements have been made and the petition served, the petitioner will produce the necessary evidence and crave sequestration. If the debtor does not appear, or does appear and cannot prove that his debts have been paid, sequestration will be awarded. Any objections are usually verbal, and the court may hear proof. Objections may be to the effect that there is a procedural defect or that there is a sequestration undischarged in another court. If there are no objections the court has no discretion and must award sequestration. The deliverance awarding sequestration is final and not subject to appeal other than by a petition for recall. A deliverance refusing sequestration may be appealed.

Recall of Sequestration (section 30)

No matter what court has awarded sequestration, application for a recall must be made to the Lord Ordinary in the Court of Session. If it is granted it restores the *status quo ante* and leaves intact all *bona fide* transactions carried through during the currency of the sequestration. The petition for recall may be made at the instance of any debtor whose estate has been sequestrated without his consent, or by the successors of any deceased debtor unless the sequestration was awarded on the application of a mandatory of the deceased debtor. It may also be at the instance of any creditor. The grounds for recall may be those which were previously advanced in opposition to the sequestration. The creditor's debt must be vouched and he will be barred if he has homologated the sequestration, *e.g.* by lodging a claim, provided always there is no radical defect in the proceedings. In the ordinary case the application must be lodged within 40 days of the deliverance awarding sequestration. It is served on the petitioner and any concurring parties and the trustee, if he has been appointed, and they are required to answer within a specific time. Notice must also be given in the EDINBURGH GAZETTE. If sequestration was awarded on the estate of a deceased debtor, and his successor was cited edictally (*i.e.* without personal or postal service upon him but merely by sending a copy of the warrant by registered post to the Keeper of Edictal Citations in Edinburgh) the application may be presented at any time before the advertisement for payment of the first dividend. Section 31 provides that nine-tenths in number and value of the creditors in the sequestration may apply for recall at any time. The court order of recall must be registered in the Register of Sequestrations and an extract in the Register of Inhibitions and Adjudications. The order itself is subject to appeal.

Grounds necessarily involving recall

Defects in the statutory requirements, provided they are clearly and specifically alleged and capable of instant verification, afford grounds on which the sequestration must be recalled.

Discretionary grounds for recall

Where the objection to the award is not apparent on the face of the proceedings the court in its discretion may refuse or grant recall. Recall has been *refused* in the following cases:—

(1) where a security by way of inhibition was not specified in the petitioning creditor's oath;

(2) where the concurring creditor was an undischarged bankrupt; and

(3) where there had been a failure to insert GAZETTE notices or otherwise carry out statutory procedure subsequent to the award.

Recall has been *granted* in the following cases:—

(1) where the sequestration was obtained by wrongful use of process;

(2) where the petitioning creditor was not put on oath by the magistrate before whom his affidavit was sworn;

(3) where it was proved that the debtor, though *ex facie* constituted notour bankrupt, was at the time really solvent in the sense of being able to meet his obligations; [7] and

(4) where there was proof of fraud of the debtor or concurring creditor, *e.g.* when the debt was not really due.

Section 43 provides that recall may be granted within three months of the date of sequestration if the majority in number and value of the creditors reside in England or Northern Ireland.

Lastly, by exercise of the *nobile officium*, the court may *annul*, rather than recall, the sequestration when it is satisfied that the interests of justice and equity justify intervention.

D—METHODS OF TERMINATING SEQUESTRATION (OTHER THAN RECALL)

(1) The Composition

Instead of winding up the estate and dividing the proceeds, the creditors, with the consent of the court, may accept an offer of composition from the bankrupt and his friends and restore him to his estate (sections 134-136). This is often the cheapest and most effective way of realising the estate, as the bankrupt may often do this with better results than an outside party. The offer of composition must be made at the first statutory meeting or at a meeting duly called for the purpose. If a majority in number and three-fourths in value of the creditors present or represented at the meeting agree to the offer being considered, the trustee must advertise it in the EDINBURGH GAZETTE for consideration at a meeting to be held after the public examination of the bankrupt. The offer must be to pay to each creditor a rateable proportion of so much per £ on his debt and all creditors must be included whether they have lodged claims or not. This procedure is essentially a matter of contract and if the offer is accepted it cannot be withdrawn without proper cause. If there is delay in carrying out the agreement, any change in circumstances during the delay may entitle the bankrupt to refuse to fulfil the offer. The change must not be due to the conduct of the bankrupt and must be of a material character. An offer must be accompanied by an offer of caution, *i.e.* a guarantee of payment. The caution must be for the full amount of the offer. The cautioner, like the bankrupt, cannot withdraw except on cause shown.

First offer

The offer may be first made at the meeting for electing the trustee (section 134), or at the meeting held after the bankrupt's

[7] *Michie* v. *Young* 1962 S.L.T. (Notes) 70.

examination or at any subsequent meeting called by the trustee with the consent of the commissioners (section 136). If the creditors agree to accept the offer they must pass a resolution to that effect by a majority in number and three-fourths in value of the creditors present at the meeting. Every creditor who has produced an affidavit may vote. If an offer has been rejected, or become ineffectual, no other offer can be entertained without the agreement in writing of nine-tenths in number and value of all the creditors (section 142).

The acceptance of the offer

Where the offer has been made at the meeting to elect the trustee, the trustee must intimate the offer in the EDINBURGH GAZETTE and advise that it will be considered after the public examination of the bankrupt, sending also a notice to all creditors claiming on the estate (sections 136 and 137). At the subsequent meeting the acceptance of the offer must be by a majority in number and three-fourths in value of the creditors present (section 135). The offer must be accepted exactly in the terms in which it is made.

When an offer is made at any meeting other than the first statutory meeting, and the creditors agree to consider it, the trustee must call another meeting not less than 21 days thereafter, and the creditors must receive at least seven days' notice. The majority required for acceptance is as mentioned above. Acceptance may be withdrawn on proof of material change of circumstances, *e.g.* where the bankrupt is discovered to have granted secret preferences. On the acceptance of the offer a bond of caution signed by the bankrupt and the proposed cautioner must be lodged with the trustee. Pending the approval of the court, the sequestration proceeds. The composition is effective when the court is satisfied and approves it as reasonable in the circumstances of the particular case (section 135). The trustee submits a report to the court, narrating the terms of the offer and the assets, the amount of the composition and caution found and provisions for necessary expenses. Also submitted are minutes of meeting and evidence that the commissioners have audited the trustee's accounts, fixing the balance due to or by him and fixing his remuneration.

Objection may be made on the ground of any irregularity in the proceedings, fraud between any of the parties, insufficiency in the amount of caution, unreasonableness of the offer or failure to pay or provide for expenses. If the court sustains any objection and does not approve the offer, it must state its grounds for rejection. If the court approves the composition, the bankrupt must make a declaration on oath in terms of section 137 " that he has made a full and fair surrender of his estate, and has not granted or promised any preference or security, or made or promised any payment, or entered into any secret or collusive agreement or transaction, to obtain the concurrence of any creditor ". The court may then grant the discharge of the bankrupt provided that there has been paid a dividend or composition of not less than 25% of all claims, or security has been found to the satisfaction of the creditors, or failure to pay that amount has, in the opinion of the court, been caused by circumstances for which the bankrupt is not responsible (section 146 (1)).

An extract of the court's deliverance granting discharge is sent to the Accountant of Court, and intimation is made also to the Register of Inhibitions and Adjudications. The discharge frees the bankrupt from all debts and obligations for which he was liable at the date of sequestration, operates as a complete discharge within the British Dominions, and revests the bankrupt in his estate, insofar as it has vested in the trustee, subject to the creditors' claims for the amount of the composition. The claims of the creditors after the discharge are converted into claims for the composition. Even if the bankrupt fails to pay the composition the claims remain for it only and if the debtor is again sequestrated the creditors can rank for it only. Under a deed of arrangement or under an extrajudicial settlement the original claims would revive. Every lawful creditor is entitled to participate in the composition. If security is held this must be deducted and the creditor can rank only on the balance. The discharge may be annulled if there has been any breach of the provisions of the Act, or if there have been preferences, payments or collusive agreements, or wilful concealment or misrepresentation of any matters which should have been reported to the creditors. If the discharge is annulled the sequestration is restored as far as possible. If the challenge is from a single creditor, the other creditors taking no part, a decree of reduction simply restores the position of the individual creditor, leaving the rights of the others unaffected. In the case of a partnership it may be stipulated that all the partners receive a discharge, or that discharge is granted only to those who offer the composition.

(2) The Deed of Arrangement

This resembles a composition contract but is more in the nature of an annulment of the sequestration proceedings. It is essentially a contract between the debtor and his creditors, the terms of which are to be agreed. Section 34 provides that at the first statutory meeting, or at any subsequent meeting called for the purpose, a majority of creditors in number or three-fourths in value may resolve that the estate be wound up by deed of arrangement. If this is done before the election of the trustee it is not necessary to proceed to an election. If the trustee has already been elected an application will be made to the court to sist proceedings for two months, and the various statutory periods will cease to run. In terms of section 35 the bankrupt must report the resolution within four days and apply for the sist. The court may hear any objections before granting the sist. The court may make reasonable arrangements for the interim preservation of the estate (section 36). No special form is prescribed for the deed of arrangement: it may provide for the realisation and distribution of the estate by the creditors themselves, or for handing it over to a trustee, or to the debtor himself on his undertaking to pay the arranged amount. If the bankrupt does not make the payment the original debt revives and the creditor may sue him for it. The deed may provide for a partial or conditional discharge of the bankrupt, or for no discharge at all. The agreed amount may be accepted by the creditors without caution, which is an essential element of the composition contract. If the sequestration has been sisted, the deed must be presented to the court for approval. If approval is granted the sequestration is at an end and the deed is binding on all creditors whether they have acceded to it or not. Section 37 provides that the provisions of the Act aimed at the prevention, challenge or setting aside of preferences shall be applied. The bankrupt should stipulate for his discharge as part of the arrangement with the creditors.

(3) Extrajudicial Settlements

These have the advantages of speed and economy; they do not require the intervention or approval of the court and may often provide a larger dividend for the creditors. They require, however, the approval, express or implied, of all the creditors, and no compulsion can be exerted on any who do not wish to accede. The debtor is not put on oath, and full co-operation on his part is therefore essential.

The two main forms of extrajudicial settlement are the trust deed and the extrajudicial composition contract.

Trust deed

In this document the debtor voluntarily gives up his estate to a named trustee to be held for its realisation and division among the creditors according to their respective rights and interests. Generally the creditor lodges a written form in which he accedes to the terms of the trust deed. Where third party security is involved the consent of the pledger or guarantor should be obtained before agreement is given by the creditor.

The terms of the trust deed will normally include clauses which—

(*a*) give authority to the trustee named in the deed to apply for sequestration (a useful sanction if the debtor does not co-operate with the trustee);

(*b*) make provision for the trustee's remuneration; and

(*c*) stipulate that, for voting and ranking, claims shall be reckoned as for sequestration and that the statutory provisions for the reduction of preferences will apply.

All creditors must be placed on an equal footing and all known creditors must accede. Often, however, the trust deed may authorise the payment in full of creditors for nominal sums. Section 185 provides that where, in the trust deed, there is no provision for the audit of a trustee's accounts and for the fixing of his fee by a committee of creditors, or where there is no committee, the Accountant of Court will be requested to audit the accounts and fix the fee. If these requirements are not satisfied the trustee will lose all right to a fee.

The trustee will be invested with full possession of the debtor's estate and he must complete his title to each asset in the appropriate manner, *e.g.*, by completion and recording of heritable title. The trustee can then realise the estate and should lodge the proceeds in a special trust account in a bank. After realisation the trustee will adjudicate on the creditors' claims and pay the dividend. He will then be entitled to his exoneration and discharge. If he cannot obtain this from the creditors he may raise in court an action of multiplepoinding and exoneration. It is useful to provide in the trust deed that creditors must deduct the value of securities held. If all creditors do not accede the debtor may apply for his sequestration. The debtor is not entitled to a discharge, unless this is provided for in the trust deed, and will remain liable for payment of debts in full. Where all creditors have acceded and the trust deed is not challenged, sequestration will be excluded.

Extrajudical composition contract

The procedure under this contract is similar to that under the judicial composition contract. Intimation of the proposed dividend is made to the creditors. A meeting is convened for consideration of the offer, and, if this is acceptable and payment of the composition is made, the debtor remains vested in his own estate. This procedure is subject to the same disadvantages as the trust deed and may be upset by any one creditor's refusing to accept and applying for sequestration. The Bankruptcy (Scotland) Act 1913 does not really have any application, and the matter is governed by the terms of agreement between debtor and creditors.

E—SEQUESTRATION PROCEEDINGS
(1) PROCEEDINGS PRIOR AND SUBSEQUENT TO THE ELECTION OF THE TRUSTEE

When the court has awarded sequestration the Act at once imposes certain duties on the party who has made the application (section 44). Within two days of the deliverance awarding sequestration an abbreviate or summary of the petition and deliverance must be presented to the Keeper of the Register of Inhibitions and Adjudications in Edinburgh (Schedule A, No. 1). The recording of the abbreviate prevents the debtor granting any deed affecting his heritable estate. The inhibition lasts five years and, if the trustee has not been discharged within that time, he must renew it (Schedule A, No. 4). Section 44 further provides that a notice in the form of Schedule B shall be inserted in the EDINBURGH GAZETTE within four days, and in the LONDON GAZETTE within six days, of the date of the deliverance awarding sequestration. Where the sequestration has been awarded in the Court of Session and transferred to the Sheriff Court, notice must be inserted in the EDINBURGH GAZETTE within six days.

The preliminary expenses of the petition and of implementing the provisions of section 44 are a proper charge on the estate and should be paid by the trustee.

Interim Preservation of the Estate (sections 14 and 15)

The court to which a petition for sequestration is presented, whether sequestration can be awarded immediately or not, may, at any time between presentation and the confirmation of the appointment of the trustee, and on the application of any creditor or *ex proprio motu*, take steps for the preservation of the estate by the appointment of a judicial factor, who must find such caution as may be deemed necessary. The judicial factor is essentially a manager who secures the estate until a trustee has been appointed. He may open lockfast places, take delivery of goods consigned to the bankrupt, and carry on an existing business. He has no general power to sell the estate, and if immediate sale were necessary he would require to seek the court's authority. He is entitled to his expenses out of the first funds available to the trustee, or from the petitioning creditor, if no trustee is appointed.

The court may also cause the books, papers, etc. of the bankrupt to be sealed up and put in safe custody, his shop or repositories to be locked until the appointment of the trustee is confirmed, or may grant warrant to take possession of assets belonging to the bankrupt and put them in safe custody (section 15). The Sheriff does not, however, have power to ordain the bankrupt to hand over money in his own possession.

Proceedings Subsequent to the Election of the Trustee

The award of sequestration gives authority for the bankrupt's estate to be ingathered and sold, and for the proceeds to be distributed among the creditors. It is necessary to consider who the creditors are, how they are convened and what are their voting powers and the nature and extent of the trustee's authority. These questions are dealt with at the first meeting of the creditors, known as " the first statutory meeting". At least six, but not more than twelve, clear days must elapse between the close of the day of the notice in the GAZETTE and the beginning of the day of the meeting (section 63). The meeting must be held in a convenient public place within the jurisdiction of the Sheriff awarding the sequestration. Section 64 lays down the procedure for the meeting. At the time and place appointed the creditors or their mandatories meet, presided over by the Sheriff or a chairman appointed by themselves and called the preses. The Sheriff must attend if two or more creditors give notice that they so wish, in which case the clerk of the meeting will be the Sheriff Clerk or his depute. If the Sheriff is not present the meeting will elect a chairman and a clerk. The creditors must produce their affidavits and claims duly sworn. The chairman will adjudicate on the claims and accord the creditors their voting rights. He must initial the affidavits, which are then transmitted to the Sheriff Clerk with the signed minute of the meeting. This is written at the meeting and should include the names and designations of the creditors and their mandatories, the amount they claim and any other facts relevant to the meeting. The bankrupt also has his obligations in connection with the first statutory meeting. Section 77 provides that he shall make up and deliver to the clerk of the meeting a written state of his affairs, specifying his whole property, wherever situated, any property in expectancy, the names of his debtors and creditors, debts due by him and to him, and a rental of his heritable property. This statement is signed by the bankrupt and delivered to the trustee, who causes it to be engrossed in the sederunt book kept by him. In the case of a partnership each partner must produce a statement of his individual affairs.

(2) THE TRUSTEE

Any creditor or his mandatory, provided he has lodged a proper affidavit and claim, is entitled to vote in the election of the trustee. He may then vote although he may be a conjunct and confident person and although his interest may be contrary to that of the general body of creditors. Section 60, however, prohibits voting by the bankrupt's wife, or any trustee for her, or any person whose debt was constituted after the date of sequestration otherwise than by succession or marriage.

The Qualification of the Trustee

The trustee is not only the manager of the bankrupt's affairs, but also the judge in the first instance of the validity of creditors' claims. He must therefore be impartial, and section 64 disqualifies the following classes of person from election:—

(1) the bankrupt himself;

(2) persons conjunct and confident with the bankrupt, including anyone who has been for a material time a professional adviser to the bankrupt;

(3) persons resident outside the jurisdiction of the Court of Session; and

(4) persons holding an adverse interest to that of the general body of creditors. That interest may not be easy to define. The mere holding of security for debt would not be a disqualification, although the valuation of the security might raise problems. It would be an adverse interest if the debt rested on a disputed claim or the creditor was claiming a challenged preference or founding on suspicious documents.

At common law the trustee may be disqualified on grounds of personal incapacity, hostility to the bankrupt, or the holding of an office inconsistent with that of trustee.

Procedure for Election

The creditors or their mandatories, having produced their affidavits and the details of these having been entered in the minutes, may proceed to elect a fit person to be trustee. No formal nomination of a candidate is required, and a contesting creditor does not require to enter in the minutes a protest that the election has resulted in favour of a particular candidate, although it is usual to do so. Only one person can be elected to act at any one time, but two or more may be elected to act in succession in the event of non-acceptance, resignation, death or disqualification of the person first elected. Once the original trustee has been elected, his election is confirmed by the Sheriff. Thereafter the office of trustee does not automatically devolve, and if another trustee is needed a new meeting must be held either to devolve the estate on the next trustee in succession or to elect a new trustee. Such a situation may arise either where the Lord Ordinary or Sheriff removes the original trustee after his election and orders a new meeting to be held, or where, if the trustee has died or been removed or has at any one time remained outwith Scotland for three months, a commissioner (see page 26) or qualified creditor applies to the Lord Ordinary or Sheriff for an order for a new meeting (section 71). Except where so authorised by statute the Sheriff has no power to call a new meeting, but the Court of Session may order a meeting where the Act makes no provision for it. At the first statutory meeting the creditors must fix the sum for which the trustee must find security for his intromissions and for the proper performance of his duties (section 69). Within seven days of the election the trustee must lodge the bond of caution, signed by himself and the cautioner, with the Sheriff Clerk. The cautioner will be liable for the trustee's intromissions even although there has been omission or negligence on the part of the creditors or of the commissioners who supervise the trustee.

Trustee's Confirmation

Although he may have been duly elected the trustee is not entitled to act until his appointment is judicially notified and confirmed. If there are any objections to his appointment the court must dispose of these before confirmation. The grounds of objection may include questions as to the validity of the votes cast, the personal qualifications of the candidate, or any irregularity in the proceedings relating to the appointment.

If the Sheriff is present at the meeting, and there are no objections stated, he must by deliverance endorsed on the minute declare the person chosen to be trustee (section 65). If there is competition, or if objections are stated to the votes or to the candidate—and these objections must be stated at the meeting—the Sheriff may decide on them immediately or make avizandum. In the latter case he may make a short note of the objections and answers and within four days he must hear the parties and declare whom he finds elected, stating his grounds for decision on each objection.

If the Sheriff has not been present at the meeting, section 66 applies. The preses of the meeting must report the proceedings to the Sheriff whether there has been a competition or not. If there is no competition or objection the Sheriff will confirm the election. Otherwise parties must lodge objections within four days and the Sheriff will adjudicate. His decision is final (section 67). The expenses of competition for the office of trustee are to be paid by the unsuccessful challenger, but not out of the bankrupt estate (section 68). When the Sheriff has confirmed the election and the trustee has lodged his bond of caution, the Sheriff Clerk issues the act and warrant (Schedule D to the Act). Within three days he will transmit a copy to the Accountant of Court, who will enter the trustee's name in the Register of Sequestrations (section 70). Section 97 provides that the act and warrant shall transfer to and vest in the trustee and his successors for behoof of the creditors the whole property of the bankrupt, both heritable and moveable, as at the date of the sequestration. The moveable estate is transferred to the same effect as if delivery or possession had been obtained or intimation made at the date of deliverance, subject always to existing preferable securities. Similar provisions apply to heritable estate.

The property affected by the act and warrant is that in which the bankrupt had a beneficial right, and not property to which he had a formal title only, because he held it in trust for third parties. Under section 97(4) any non-vested contingent right of succession or interest in property conceived in favour of the bankrupt under a will or marriage settlement vests in the trustee as if it had been assigned at the date of sequestration, subject again to valid preferable securities. The trustee may require to register his title, *e.g.* in the case of shares in companies, ships, patents, trade-marks, etc., before it will become effectual and able to resist any challenge.

The trustee takes the property *tantum et tale* as it was held by the bankrupt. That means that both the extent and the quality of his right are identical with that of the bankrupt. He cannot maintain a right which would be reducible on the grounds of the bankrupt's fraud.

The trustee is not entitled to the tools of the bankrupt's trade, or to alimentary funds, although he may apply to the court to have the latter reduced to a reasonable level and the balance paid to him.

The trustee must, within ten days of the confirmation of his appointment, register his act and warrant in the Register of Inhibitions and Adjudications to acquire a good and complete title to the bankrupt's heritable estate subject to existing charges. Even when unrecorded the act and warrant is a valid link in title to heritable property.

Acquirenda

Any estate falling to or acquired by the bankrupt after the date of sequestration and before the date of his discharge falls under the sequestration. Section 98 provides that the *acquirenda* shall vest in the trustee as at the date of acquisition, but to complete his title the trustee must petition the court in an action of declarator. Until the title is complete the *acquirenda* are liable to the diligence of creditors whose debts are subsequent to the sequestration. The court will appoint intimation in the GAZETTE and a time for representations. If the time expires and no contrary interest is expressed the court will declare the *acquirenda* to belong to the trustee. The bankrupt must notify *acquirenda* to the trustee and if he does not do so will lose his benefits under the Act.

All acts and payments by the bankrupt after the date of sequestration and before the date of discharge are void apart from the following exceptions (section 107):—

(1) where the bankrupt has delivered goods to a *bona fide* purchaser who was ignorant of the sequestration and who has paid the price, the purchaser need not restore the goods;

(2) if a debtor, while in ignorance of the sequestration, has made a *bona fide* payment to the bankrupt he need not pay again to the trustee; and

(3) if the possessor of a bill or promissory note payable by the bankrupt has, in ignorance of the sequestration, received payment from the bankrupt and given up the bill, he is not liable to make repayment to the trustee unless the trustee restores him to his prior position and frees him from loss or damage.

Regarding the vesting of the estate, there are four points to notice in connection with particular property:—

(1) The trustee has a right of action in the courts and may sue for recovery of any property or of any debt due to the bankrupt as the bankrupt would have done but for his sequestration; if the bankrupt has already raised the action the trustee may be sisted as a party and will normally be so sisted if there is a chance of increasing the trust estate. This power would not apply to personal actions, *e.g.* of divorce.

(2) The trustee is not bound to take up contracts which are of an onerous or speculative nature. He may abandon an action already begun, subject to the other party's right to lodge any claims arising from it, but he must intimate within a reasonable time whether or not he intends to make himself a party to the action.

(3) Property held in trust by the bankrupt does not pass to the trustee but, if it is so inmixed with his own funds as to be undistinguishable, the beneficiaries of the trust funds can rank as ordinary creditors only.

(4) Policies of assurance under the Married Women's Policies of Assurance (Scotland) Act 1880 effected by a married man on his own life for the benefit of his wife and children are protected from creditors. Where, however, a policy is effected to defraud creditors, or within two years of bankruptcy, the creditors may claim repayment of the premiums paid.

The Removal and Resignation of the Trustee

(1) Under section 71 a majority in number and value of creditors present at any meeting called for the purpose may remove the trustee or accept his resignation. No reason need be given and any appeal to the court must be on the validity of the votes and regularity of the proceedings and not the merits of the decision.

(2) Again under section 71, the Lord Ordinary or Sheriff may remove the trustee on the application of one-fourth in value of the creditors entitled to vote. After service on the trustee and intimation in the GAZETTE the petitioners must show cause for removal. After removal the court may appoint a meeting to devolve the succession upon the trustee next in line or to appoint a new trustee.

(3) Any one creditor, or the Accountant of Court, may petition for the removal of the trustee on the grounds of his failure to lodge the annual return prescribed by section 157, or where the Accountant of Court reports that his duties are being improperly performed (section 158).

The trustee may not resign without the consent of a majority in number and value of the creditors at a meeting called to receive his resignation, which, as in the case of removal, will be followed by procedure for his replacement.

(3) THE COMMISSIONERS

These are a representative body of creditors who are appointed to join the trustee and assist him in the management of the estate. They are generally three in number (section 72) and they act gratuitously. They are elected at the first statutory meeting immediately after the election of the trustee and they do not require to find caution. The Sheriff decides who is elected and the election is recorded in the sederunt book. A majority of commissioners is a quorum, but if only two have been elected they must concur. No person is eligible as a commissioner who is disqualified from being a trustee (section 72), although the common law rules of disqualification are not applied with the same stringency. A commissioner may resign office at any time. There are three modes of removal of a commissioner from office:—

(1) where the mandatory of a creditor has been elected he will lose office if his principal gives written notice to the trustee that he has recalled the mandate (this intimation must be recorded in the sederunt book);

(2) a majority of creditors in value at any meeting called for the purpose may remove one commissioner and elect another in his place; and

(3) any creditor may complain to the Accountant of Court that a commissioner has not observed his statutory duties, and if the Accountant reports this to the court the Lord Ordinary or Sheriff may remove the commissioner from office.

Where a casual vacancy occurs the trustee should call a meeting to fill it.

The Functions of the Commissioners

The commissioners superintend the actings of the trustee, concur with him in his intromissions and transactions, advise and assist in the management of the estate and decide as to paying or postponing a dividend (section 81). On giving prior notice to the trustee, they may call a meeting of creditors (section 93). They have a right of access at all reasonable times to the documents of the sequestration in the possession of the trustee (section 80). Section 121 directs that within fourteen days after the expiry of four months from the date of award of sequestration the commissioners shall hold a meeting in order to—

(1) examine the state of affairs made up by the trustee and examine and docquet his account of intromissions;

(2) ascertain whether he has lodged in bank the money he has recovered, debiting him with interest at 20% on all sums over £50 not so lodged;

(3) audit the trustee's accounts and certify in the sederunt book the balance due to or by him;

(4) fix the trustee's commission and authorise him to take credit for it; and

(5) declare the first dividend, having made reasonable provision for contingencies.

A similar procedure applies to subsequent dividends also.

The commissioners may not purchase any part of the bankrupt's estate (section 116). The concurrence of the commissioners is required before the trustee can demand the conveyance of a security from a creditor, settle preferential debts without formal oaths having been lodged, or pay dividends. The trustee will not be relieved of liability in any respect merely because he has had the sanction of the commissioners.

(4) THE POSITION OF THE BANKRUPT

When the trustee has had an opportunity of considering the bankrupt's state of affairs, a diet is fixed for the public examination of the bankrupt. The trustee must apply to the Sheriff for a diet within eight days from the date of his act and warrant. The Sheriff orders the bankrupt to appear not sooner than seven or later than fourteen days from the date of the warrant (section 83). Intimation is made in the EDINBURGH GAZETTE and to all creditors who have lodged claims or who have been disclosed in the state of affairs made by the bankrupt under section 77. The examination is conducted on oath, and the Sheriff may grant a warrant for the arrest of the bankrupt if he does not appear (section 84). He may also order the examination of the bankrupt's wife, family or other persons who can give information (section 86). In terms of section 87 the bankrupt or others cited must answer all lawful questions relevant to the bankrupt's affairs and, if so ordered, deliver documents to the trustee for inspection. The law of evidence is not applied strictly and the Sheriff may exercise a wide discretion in allowing or rejecting questions. The examination is under oath or affirmation (section 88) and takes place before the Sheriff except where a commission is granted to take the examination elsewhere. The evidence will be recorded by a shorthand writer. The examination may be held in open court or in private. The examination may be adjourned for a brief interval, but not to allow a creditor a chance to test the veracity of the bankrupt's statements.[8] The Sheriff may on the application of the trustee order as many diets of re-examination as may seem necessary (sections 84 and 86). The questions may be put by the Sheriff or, with his permission, by any creditor (section 89). The trustee cannot object to a question, if it is otherwise competent, on the grounds that it may prove injurious to the general body of creditors. The decision of the Sheriff on the competency of a question may be appealed to the Court of Session within eight days. If the bankrupt refuses to be sworn or to answer a question or to produce documents he may be imprisoned until he complies. Before his examination is closed he may make such alterations or additions to his written state of affairs as he considers fit. The state of affairs is then subscribed by the Sheriff and the bankrupt, who also takes the oath in terms of section 91, and the oath is engrossed in the sederunt book.

The Rights of the Bankrupt

(1) Under the Act the bankrupt may apply for or oppose his sequestration, or apply for its recall; he may report to the creditors a decision to wind up the estate under a deed of arrangement; he may call on the trustees and commissioners to give an account of their management, amend his state of affairs, make composition offers and, in certain circumstances, apply for his discharge.

(2) He may continue to carry on business or enter any new trade or business, although he commits an offence if he obtains credit for more than £10 without disclosing that he is an undischarged bankrupt (section 182). Sequestration does not affect his holding office as executor, etc., but generally he is debarred from holding public office.

(3) Although the award of sequestration deprives the bankrupt of his property, the radical right in his estate remains in him and he may therefore claim an accounting from the trustee and also claim any part of the estate abandoned by the creditors (section 138).

[8] *Unger* v. *Blogg* (1867) 5 M. 1049.

Generally the bankrupt cannot insist in any action if the trustee refuses to take it up, unless it is of a purely personal nature. In most actions at the instance of the bankrupt he will be ordered to find caution for expenses. Under section 74 the creditors may grant an allowance to the bankrupt, it being reasonable that he be maintained while affording assistance to the creditors. At any meeting four-fifths in value of the creditors may determine the amount of this allowance. It may be continued until the period allowed for the second dividend, and in special cases thereafter if it is in the interests of the estate. When the sequestration is at an end the bankrupt's radical right revives as an active title to sue.

Fees or emoluments which are the result of the bankrupt's personal labour or skill do not fall to the trustee, but if the bankrupt holds a salaried office the trustee may demand the salary and allot a proportion back to him. Alimentary funds are not attached unless the court considers them excessive.

The Liabilities of the Bankrupt

The bankrupt is liable to actions at the instance of his creditors for obligations contracted prior to and subsequent to his sequestration. These actions are of little practical avail, and decree does not entitle the creditor to be ranked on the estate. The bankrupt is liable to personal diligence at the instance of the Crown for fines, taxes, etc., and at the instance of local authorities for payment of rates. He may be imprisoned for crime, offences under the Act, or wilful failure to pay under a decree for aliment.

(5) REALISATION AND SALE OF THE ESTATE

As soon as possible after his appointment the trustee must take possession of the bankrupt's estate and make an inventory and valuation, a copy of which must be sent to the Accountant of Court (section 71). He must thereafter manage, realise and recover the bankrupt's estate and convert it into money according to the directions by the creditors given at any meeting, or, failing such directions, with the advice of the commissioners (section 78). At the second meeting of creditors the trustee must submit his report with his explanations. The creditors may then give directions for the management of the estate. If they do not give directions it is the duty of the trustee to proceed on the advice of the commissioners. In the absence of directions from the creditors it is not competent for the trustee or commissioners to apply to the court for guidance.

A resolution of the creditors may be appealed at the instance of any one creditor or of the bankrupt.

Although it is the intention of the Act that the estate be converted into money as soon as possible, immediate realisation may result in loss: it may be profitable to carry on a business and it may be expedient for the trustees to employ the bankrupt in this connection.

Sale of Heritable Estate

This may be effected by a public voluntary sale or by private bargain. In the former case the sale is by auction. The trustee, with the consent of the commissioners, will fix the upset price, and the property must then be sold for not less than the price fixed. If no sale results it may be exposed again at a reduced upset price. The disposition is granted by the trustee with the consent of the commissioners. If heritable creditors are involved, the upset price must be sufficient to cover their principal debt, with interest and expenses (section 110). In terms of section 111 the trustee may sell by private bargain, provided he has the concurrence of the majority of the creditors in number and value, of any heritable creditors, and the Accountant of Court. A private sale by the trustee alone would be invalid. Where there are several heritable creditors over the estate to be sold the trustee must prepare a scheme of ranking on the price obtained and present it to the court for approval. Judgment on this scheme is warrant against the purchaser of the heritable estate for payment of the price.

Sale of Moveable Estate

There are no express provisions for such sales in the Act, although from the terms of section 133 it seems that a sale by public auction is envisaged. With the consent of the commissioners, the trustee may sell moveables by private bargain (with the exception of book debts). If twelve months from the first deliverance the trustee and commissioners consider it advisable to realise the outstanding estate, they must, under section 133, fix a meeting of creditors to consider the matter. The meeting is advertised in the GAZETTE, and notice, with valuations etc., given to creditors. If a majority in value of the creditors so decide, the trustee must proceed to sale by auction after one month's notice. Section 102 regulates the terms on which copyright interests may be sold.

(6) VOTING RIGHTS OF CREDITORS

At all meetings of creditors questions are decided by a majority in value of those present and entitled to vote, except where special majorities are required (section 96). If creditors are required to be reckoned by number no creditor whose claim is for less than £20 is counted, although such may be included in a computation for value. Voting rights are determined by the preses of the meeting, not by the trustee. A creditor may vote even though an objection to his claim is under consideration by the court. Where a creditor holds a security he must, before voting, make an oath in which he must put a value on the security, deduct this value from his debt, and specify the balance. If the security subjects are sold, he must specify the free proceeds and deduct them from his debt (section 55). The creditor is entitled to vote in respect of the balance only, without prejudice to the amount of his debt in other respects. In questions relating to the management or disposal of the estate over which he holds the security, however, the creditor is entitled to vote for the full amount.

In terms of section 56 the creditor must in a similar way put a value on the obligation of any co-obligant and deduct it from his debt. If the bankrupt is liable as a cautioner, the creditor must value and deduct the obligation of the principal debtor. A creditor in a debt owed by a partnership is not bound to deduct for voting purposes the value which he may be entitled to claim upon the estates of the individual partners. In claiming on a partner's estate he must, however, value and deduct his claims against other partners, in so far as they are liable in an obligation of relief (section 57). The trustee may require a creditor holding a security to grant a conveyance or assignation thereof on the payment of the value specified in his oath, plus 20% in addition to this value (section 58). The trustee, with the consent of the commissioners, may make this requirement within two months after the creditor has used his oath in voting at any meeting, or else this requirement may be made by a majority of the other creditors. The creditor may correct his valuation by a new oath and deduct this new value from his debt at any time after the lapse of 21 days from the date on which the claim has been voted on and before the trustee has required him to convey the asset held in security.

Contingent Creditors

Such creditors may not petition for sequestration or concur in such a process. If the contingency can be valued at the date of lodging the claim, the creditor may elect to have his claim valued and may vote on the valued amount. Where the contingent claim cannot be valued he may have a dividend set aside for him on the full amount, to await purification of the contingency. Section 49 provides the procedure for valuation. Notice is given to the bankrupt and to the petitioning or concurring creditor; application is then made to the trustee (or, if there is no trustee, to the Sheriff) to value the debt. The method of valuation is in the discretion of the trustee, or Sheriff, as the case may be. The judgment of the Sheriff can be appealed to the Court of Session within eight days, and that of the trustee to the Sheriff within 14 days. Pending the appeal, the creditor may vote on his claim as valued. If the creditor elects to await the contingency he may not vote in the interval. If the claim has been valued for voting it may be revalued for ranking. If this has not been done the trustee must make reasonable provision for payment of a dividend when the contingency has occurred. No creditor in respect of an annuity granted by the bankrupt can vote or draw a dividend until the annuity has been valued (section 50).

The Sheriff or trustee may call on a creditor to rectify the oath and claim which has been produced for the purpose of voting, ranking or drawing a dividend, and failing rectification the claim will be disallowed. If the oath and claim has been made fraudulently or improperly then rectification need not be permitted (section 47).

(7) RANKING OF CLAIMS AND PAYMENT OF DIVIDENDS

When the whole estate has been realised and necessary charges and the trustee's fee paid, the balance forms a fund for division " among those who were creditors of the bankrupt at the date of the sequestration, ranked according to their several rights and interests " (section 117). The necessary charges include the expenses incurred by the petitioning or concurring creditor prior to the election of the trustee, and the expenses of management, including all debts properly charged against the trustee.

The Trustee's State of Funds

Within 14 days after the expiry of four months from the date of the deliverance awarding sequestration, the trustee must make up a state of the whole estate of the bankrupt, of the funds recovered, and of the property not yet recovered, with all necessary explanations and a general account of his management. Within a like period the commissioners must complete their audit of the trustee's accounts and declare what is available for payment of a dividend after allowing for contingencies (section 121).

In terms of sections 127 and 129 a similar procedure is followed every four months with a view to making payment of subsequent dividends.

Ranking Rights of Creditors

An affidavit and claim is necessary to enable a creditor to rank, and this is similar to that used for the purposes of petitioning and voting. In these two cases, however, the claim need only be *ex facie* valid, while in questions of ranking the creditor must satisfy the standard of proof which would be required in a court action. A claim which is rejected for a preferential ranking may be admitted to an ordinary ranking. Where a creditor lodges a claim for an ordinary ranking, and the trustee knows that the creditor is entitled to a preference, the former must order the latter to amend his claim so that he can be ranked according to his rights.

Time for Lodging Claims

In terms of section 119, to participate in payment of the first dividend, the creditor must have produced his affidavit at least two months before the date fixed for payment of the dividend, the period being one month in the case of subsequent dividends. If a creditor lodges a claim too late to participate in a particular dividend but in time for a subsequent dividend, the claimant is entitled to receive out of the first of the funds an equalising dividend.

Securities

A creditor holding security for his claim must, for the purpose of ranking for dividend, put a value on his security and deduct it from the debt (section 61), and the trustee may call for a conveyance of the security on payment of the value specified. The creditor will rank for the balance of his debt. The trustee must exercise his option to purchase within a reasonable time. While collateral securities are valued and deducted for voting purposes, they are not required to be valued or deducted for ranking for dividend because the co-obligant is not the bankrupt, and the security is not over the bankrupt's estate. A creditor in right of such claims can draw a dividend on the several estates provided he does not draw in aggregate more than the full value of his claims. The rule that there can be no double ranking in a sequestration for the same debt is strictly applied.

Trustee's Adjudication on Claims

At any time after a claim has been lodged the trustee may require further evidence in support of the claim. If a dividend is to be paid, the trustee must, within the 14 days specified in section 121 as the time within which the commissioners must examine his report, examine the claims. If he does not require further evidence he must admit or reject the claims. In his deliverance he must give his reasons for any rejection. He will make up a list of creditors entitled to a dividend, specifying the amount of the debt, with interest to the date of sequestration, and whether the claims are preferable, ordinary or contingent. He must also prepare a list of claims which he has rejected (section 123).

When a dividend is to be paid the trustee must advertise in the GAZETTE the time and place of payment within eight days after the expiry of the 14-day period already mentioned (section 124). Notices must also be posted to the creditors, including those whose claims have been rejected. The trustee's deliverance on a claim can be appealed within 14 days of the publication in the GAZETTE of the notice of payment. Failing appeal, the deliverance becomes final and conclusive. A rejection does not, however, preclude the lodging of a new claim for participation in subsequent dividends.

Payment of Dividends

The first dividend is to be paid on the first lawful day after the expiry of six months from the date of the deliverance awarding sequestration (section 126). Within 14 days after the expiry of eight months from such deliverance the second dividend should be provided for (section 127), and it should be paid on the first lawful day after the expiry of ten months from the deliverance (section 128). Subsequent dividends are to be paid on the first lawful day after the expiry of three months from the date of payment of the preceding dividend. With the consent of the Accountant of Court, the trustee may accelerate the payment of any dividend, provided that the first dividend is paid not earlier than four months from the date of sequestration. Where payment of a dividend is accelerated, any other matters which are affected thereby may also be accelerated (section 130).

The commissioners may postpone payment of a dividend from one statutory period to another provided that appropriate notice is given in the GAZETTE (section 131). In cases of exceptional delay the trustee and the commissioners may petition the court for such alteration as is necessary.

Ranking

Creditors are ranked according to their classes in the following order:—

(1) preferred creditors;

(2) ordinary creditors;

(3) contingent creditors; and

(4) postponed creditors.

(1) *Preferred creditors*

This class is divided in turn into *secured* and *privileged* creditors. *Secured* creditors are entitled to look to their security for the satisfaction or part satisfaction of their claims. If the security is more than sufficient, the balance must be made over to the trustee. The award of sequestration renders the right of set off instantly enforceable, and bankers may therefore apply credit balances to the reduction or extinction of overdrafts, ranking for any balance according to the circumstances. There are several debts which are *privileged* and which, although no security attaches to them, are to be met in full before other creditors are paid. These include death-bed and funeral expenses and the expense of suitable mournings for the family of the deceased. In terms of section 35, Friendly Societies Act 1896, if an officer has at the date of his bankruptcy possession of funds belonging to such a society, the trustee in bankruptcy must return them on the request of two trustees of the society. Section 118 [9] specifies certain classes of debts to which a statutory preference is given:—

(*a*) all poor or local rates and taxes for not more than one year;

(*b*) payments due to the Crown for taxes not exceeding one year's assessment;

(*c*) wages or salaries of clerks, servants or workmen for a period of four months prior to sequestration, including holiday pay, accrued holiday pay and pay during absence through sickness, not exceeding £200 in any one case;

(*d*) National Insurance contributions for the year preceding sequestration; and

(*e*) sums due as compensation under a variety of statutes, particularly in the field of employment.

[9] As amended by section 115, Companies Act 1947, and sections 71 and 90, National Insurance (Industrial Injuries) Act 1946 and sections 55 (2) and 79 (*f*), National Insurance Act 1946.

Privileged debts rank equally among themselves and are to be paid in full unless funds are insufficient, in which case they are to be abated in equal proportions. With the consent of the commissioners, the trustee may dispense with the lodging of affidavits in connection with those debts and also make payment before the date of payment of the first dividend.

(2) and (3) *Ordinary and contingent creditors*

These rank equally on the estate after the claims of the preferred creditors have been satisfied. Contingent creditors will not of course receive payment until the contingency occurs, but the trustee must set aside funds to meet the claims when they materialise.

(4) *Postponed creditors*

These will rank only when creditors of all the other classes have been paid in full. They include married women whose funds have been intermingled with those of their husbands, and persons who lent money to a business in consideration of receiving a share in the profits or a rate of interest varying with the profits of the business.

Unclaimed Dividends

Before the trustee can obtain his discharge he must send the sederunt book to the Accountant of Court, who will direct him to lodge all unclaimed dividends in the bank (section 153 (1)). After the discharge of the trustee, and within seven years of such lodging of unclaimed dividends, any party proving his right will receive payment of such dividend. After seven years of such lodging any dividends still unclaimed are forfeited to the Queen's and Lord Treasurer's Remembrancer.

(8) DISCHARGES

Discharge of the Bankrupt

This is now regarded almost as a matter of right, provided the statutory requirements are observed and the bankrupt has not acted improperly in any way. The application should be made by the bankrupt himself, or his mandatory or representative, to the Lord Ordinary or Sheriff, advertised in the GAZETTE, and intimated to each known creditor, whether he has lodged a claim or not (section 143). The application is competent—

(1) at any time after the second statutory meeting, provided every creditor who has duly produced his oath concurs;

(2) on the expiry of six months from the date of the deliverance awarding sequestration, provided a majority in number and four-fifths in value of the creditors concur;

(3) on the expiry of twelve months provided a majority in number and two-thirds in value of the creditors concur;

(4) on the expiry of 18 months, provided a majority in number and value of the creditors concur; or

(5) on the expiry of two years without the consent of the creditors.

Where necessary, the creditors' concurrence must be obtained before the presentation of the petition. The petition must be expressed in writing and refer to the trustee's report on the bankrupt's conduct. The minutes of a meeting at which all creditors have consented will be sufficient. The trustee will generally certify the consents before the presentation of the petition but his certificate is not conclusive and will not bar him from objecting to the discharge.

Trustee's Report

The bankrupt may not petition for his discharge or obtain the consent of any creditor until the trustee has prepared a report stating whether—

(1) the bankrupt has made fair disclosure and surrender of his estate;

(2) he has attended the diet of examination;

(3) he has been guilty of any collusion; and

(4) his bankruptcy has arisen from innocent misfortune and losses in business or from culpable and undue conduct.

The report must be prepared by the trustee on the requisition of the bankrupt, which cannot be made within five months of the first deliverance. The report is *prima facie*, but not conclusive, evidence of the facts contained in it. It must be read to the creditors but they may not pass a resolution disapproving it. Where there is no opposition to the petition the court will issue after 21 days a deliverance finding the bankrupt entitled to his discharge, subject to section 146 (1), which provides that a bankrupt will not be entitled to his discharge unless he has paid a dividend of at least 25% of all claims or has found security for that amount, or alternatively, in the opinion of the court, failure to do so has arisen from circumstances for which the bankrupt is not responsible.

Any creditor may object to the petition on the following grounds:

(1) material defects in the statutory procedure for the petition for discharge;

(2) failure by the bankrupt to comply with any of the duties imposed on him by statute;

(3) the granting of preferences by the bankrupt, or his entering into collusive agreements for obtaining a discharge (section 150); or

(4) extravagant and reckless trading by the bankrupt.

The judgment of the creditors will not be lightly set aside by the court.

The court may impose conditions on the grant of discharge, and its decision is not subject to appeal. If the bankrupt is found entitled to his discharge he must make a declaration or oath that he has made a full and fair surrender of his estate and that he has not granted or promised any preference, or made any collusive agreement to obtain a creditor's concurrence (section 144). If the court is satisfied, it will pronounce the final order discharging the bankrupt. An extract of the order is sent to the Accountant of Court. The court's decision may be appealed. The order frees the bankrupt from all debts and obligations for which he was liable at the date of his sequestration, but not from debts or penalties due to the Crown.

Discharge of the Trustee

In the ordinary course the sequestration continues until the trustee also is discharged. The trustee may apply for his discharge after the final division of the funds. In terms of section 152 he must, by advertisement in the GAZETTE, call a meeting of creditors to be held not sooner than 14 days after such publication. Circulars must also be sent to every creditor who has lodged an affidavit and claim. At the meeting, known as the third statutory meeting, the trustee lays before the creditors the sederunt book, accounts and lists of unclaimed dividends, and the creditors may " declare their opinion of his conduct as trustee ", although this is not essential.

After the meeting the trustee will present to the court a petition for discharge, and after its consideration and the hearing of any creditor the court may pronounce a decree of exoneration. Intimation of the petition will be made to any creditor who objects at the meeting, and to the Accountant of Court, whom the court may occasionally ask to lodge a report.

The extract of the decree of exoneration is transmitted to the Accountant of Court and entered in the Register of Sequestrations, and the trustee's bond of caution is delivered up.

The discharge may be set aside if it is proved that it was obtained by fraud, but such application would require to be made within a reasonable time.

F—SUMMARY SEQUESTRATION

This is a simplified form of process applicable where the debtor's assets do not exceed £300, and the details of the procedure may be found in sections 174-177.

Index

Cases Cited

Printed by William Blackwood & Sons Ltd., Edinburgh